Read-Aloud Plays

IMMIGRATION

by

Sarah Glasscock

SCHOLASTIC
PROFESSIONAL BOOKS

New York • Toronto • London • Auckland • Sydney • Mexico City • New Delhi • Hong Kong

A very special thanks to Barbara Bedway for sharing
her grandmother, and to Elmer Luke

Cover design by Pamela Simmons

Interior design by Melinda Belter

Interior illustrations by Teresa Southwell

ISBN 0-590-64458-0

Table of CONTENTS

Introduction

AN OVERVIEW OF IMMIGRATION TO AMERICA

America is a land of immigrants. According to the 1992 census, more than 30 different ethnic designations were named by more than 100,000 Americans. The census recorded 58 million German Americans, 39 million Irish Americans, 33 million English Americans, 30 million African Americans, 22 million Hispanic Americans, 15 million Italian Americans, 10 million French Americans, and 9 million Polish Americans. The very first census in the United States was taken in 1790. About 1 million African Americans and 4 million European Americans were recorded. This marked the turning point; people who arrived in America after this date were no longer colonists, they were immigrants. In most cases, the promise of freedom—religious, political, social, and economic—has drawn immigrants to these shores. The African American experience, however, has been vastly different from that of other immigrant groups. They didn't come here voluntarily.

The United States officially began recording immigration statistics in 1820. This country has experienced three great waves of immigration. The first wave, often known as the Old Immigrants, occurred between 1820 to 1890. Most of these immigrants came from northern and western Europe. The Irish were fleeing famine; German Jews sought religious freedom; German and Scandinavian farmers settled in the Great Plains; and the Chinese entering from the west were lured by the Gold Rush. During these years, only the Civil War slowed down immigration.

The second wave, the Great Migration, lasted from 1890 to 1924. Southern and eastern Europeans poured into Ellis Island in New York Harbor. So did Russian Jews who were escaping pogroms in the Pale of Settlement. On the West Coast, Japanese were arriving at Angel Island. Again, war intervened to stop the flow of immigrants into this country. At the end of World War I, refugees flooded into the United States, where unemployment was high. In 1924, quotas were placed on the number of immigrants who could come to America.

The third wave of immigrants arrived in the United States after World War II and included refugees from Vietnam, Laos, Cambodia, and Cuba. During this

time period, Central and South Americans headed north for economic and political reasons.

No matter where they emigrated from, people's stories often have striking similarities—the separation of families, long and difficult passages across the sea, crowded living conditions in the cities, hard work, and discrimination. But everyone's story, too, is unique as a rich tradition of oral histories testifies. To really understand what it's like to be an American, let your students immerse themselves in these voices from the past.

A DESCRIPTION OF THE TEACHING GUIDES

Each play is followed by a teaching guide that contains background information, a bibliography, and six activities. The background information for each group of immigrants focuses primarily on the historical context surrounding the play. In most cases, the time period covered coincides with the greatest influx of each immigrant group into the United States. A variety of fiction and nonfiction books appear in the bibliography. The background information and bibliography may be shared with students either before or after they read the plays. The cross-curricular activities fall into three categories—discussion, writing, and research—and emphasize individual work as well as cooperative learning. Feel free to alter the activities to meet the particular needs of your own students' interests and learning styles.

PERFORMING THE PLAYS

These plays can work on many levels. Students can sit at their desks and read aloud their roles, or they can perform the plays in front of the class. To increase their interest, suggest adding props, costumes, and sets. Students who don't feel comfortable performing will be able to participate in behind-the-scenes roles. Emphasize nontraditional casting. Let girls take on male roles and vice versa. Your class may not have a Czech American to play Grace Malina or an Arab American to play Wedad Habib in "A Pack Full of Dreams." Remind your students that role playing, stepping into someone else's shoes, is what plays are all about. In time, you and your class may want to tackle a full-scale production of one of the plays in the school auditorium. Enlist parents to help with costumes, sound, lighting, sets, publicity, and programs. Invite the school and community to celebrate America's diversity with your class.

Leaving Hunger Behind

CAST OF CHARACTERS
(in order of appearance)

Granny Collins: Nora O'Keefe's grandmother

Nora O'Keefe: 17-year-old girl who immigrates to America

Joseph O'Keefe: Nora's younger brother

Bridget O'Keefe: Nora's younger sister

Mary O'Keefe: Nora's mother

Bill Quinn: Neighbor

Michael O'Keefe: Nora's father

Ann Marie Dolan: Neighbor

Madelon Carty: Neighbor; Nora's best friend

Runners 1-2: Con men who try to took advantage of arriving immigrants

Rosalie O'Keefe: Nora's aunt who lives in Boston

Kathleen Maguire: Cook

Alice Hastings: Boston woman who hires Nora as a servant

ACT 1

Scene: 1850, in a village in County Galway, Ireland. A going-away party is being held in the O'Keefes' home for their daughter Nora, who is leaving for America. The one-room house is made of sod; the floor is dirt, and the roof is thatched.

GRANNY COLLINS: You've got enough food, haven't you, Nora? You'll be on the ship for two months, maybe more. I can let go a few more potatoes—

NORA O'KEEFE: I've enough potatoes, Granny. You mustn't give up any more of your potatoes. You've little enough as it is.

GRANNY COLLINS: Oh, I'm an old woman. Old women don't need to eat so much. But you, you're starting on a grand adventure. You'll need fortifying.

JOSEPH O'KEEFE: Here now! What's all this seriousness? No seriousness allowed! This is a send-off for our Nora. Why, Granny, don't you know she'll be back in five years, wearing feathers in her hair and tossing gold coins right and left?

GRANNY COLLINS (*outraged*): Feathers in her hair! No granddaughter of mine—oh, Joseph O'Keefe, you've a wicked tongue in your head, teasing me like that.

(*Joseph and Granny walk off, arm in arm. Bridget rushes up and takes Nora's arm.*)

BRIDGET O'KEEFE: I don't want you to go!

NORA O'KEEFE: I have to, you know that. It's the only way. There'll be one less mouth to feed here, and I'll be making enough money in America to help out.

BRIDGET O'KEEFE: You'll be making enough money in America to send a ticket back for me, you mean. Well, what if I don't want to go to America? Have you never thought of that? Send all the money you like, but I won't go! I won't!

MARY O'KEEFE: Here, here, what's all this? We've guests in our home.

BRIDGET O'KEEFE: I'm not going to America!

MARY O'KEEFE: If it's a choice between staying here and starving or going to America, you'll be going to America, my girl. One day, *I'll* be going to America, so will your Da and your brother Joseph. Look out the door. What have we got here? A field full of rotten potatoes. A field that we don't own— that we'll never own.

BILL QUINN: Did you hear, Kitty Deazy, sick with the fever, got put out of her house. Her a widow with three small ones, all of them sick with the fever, too. The landlord cut her wheat, sold it, then tore down her house so his cattle could have more pasture. They were tearing the thatch off the roof while Dan Conlan was carrying poor Kitty out the door.

MICHAEL O'KEEFE: The landlords won't stop until they've kicked all the Irish out of their homes.

ANN MARIE DOLAN: They won't stop until they've kicked all of the Irish out of Ireland. You wait and see.

MARY O'KEEFE (*clapping her hands*): Here, here, nobody invited the English in. This is a party for my oldest girl. Bill Quinn, if you want to work your mouth, give us a song.

(*Bill Quinn pulls out a harmonica, and all the guests except Nora and Madelon crowd around him.*)

MADELON CARTY: You'll write to me, won't you? You promise?

NORA O'KEEFE: Every week, I promise.

MADELON CARTY: Are you scared?

NORA O'KEEFE: Scared? No. What's to be scared of? My very own room in a warm house where there's plenty of food to eat? Working inside instead of having to go out into the field and dig rotten potatoes and cut up sod to burn in the fireplace?

MADELON CARTY: Scared that you might not ever see us again?

NORA O'KEEFE: No, because that's not going to happen. Aunt Rosy's sent for me. I'll send for Bridget. We'll all send for Mother and Father and Joseph. Then we'll make enough money to buy our land from the English, and back here we'll be.

MADELON CARTY: You won't be back. I'll never see you again, I know that. This isn't a going-away party. You know what they call this, don't you? It's an American wake, because everybody knows that we'll never see you again. When you leave tomorrow, it'll be just like you died.

ACT 2

Scene 1: Two months later at a Boston wharf where Nora's ship has docked. Nora is looking around the crowded wharf for her aunt. The two runners make their move toward her.

RUNNER 1 (*trying to grab Nora's bag*): Here all alone are you, miss? Let me give you a hand with your belongings.

NORA O'KEEFE (*holding on to her bag*): No, thank you. I've heard about the likes of you. Trying to take advantage of us just arriving.

RUNNER 2 (*reaching for Nora's bag from the other side*): That's right, miss. Can't be too careful. You'll be wanting a decent place to stay. You just follow me, and I'll take good care of you—

NORA O'KEEFE (*swinging her bag at both of the runners*): Mind your hands, both of you, or I'll see to it that you need taking care of.

ROSALIE O'KEEFE (*hurrying through the crowd*): Nora! Nora! Stay right where you are!

(*The two runners disappear into the crowd. Nora and Rosalie hug.*)

NORA O'KEEFE: I'm so glad to be here. But I still feel like I'm rolling around on that ship.

ROSALIE O'KEEFE: Look at you. Oh, my poor girl, you're so thin. Come along, we'll get a good, hot meal into you . . . and a bath, before you meet your employers.

NORA O'KEEFE (*hanging back, suddenly shy*): But Aunt Rosy, what am I to do? This is a city. I'm nothing but a farm girl used to digging in the fields.

ROSALIE O'KEEFE: You're a smart girl is what you are, Nora O'Keefe. You'll learn fast, you'll see. Besides, once Mrs. Hastings sees what beautiful lace those hands of yours can make, she'll be keeping you busy, don't you worry now. (*hugging Nora again*) Oh, do tell me about the family. How's my brother? How's your mother? Any word from your brother Sean in Australia? We're truly a spread-out family now, aren't we?

Scene 2: Later that day, in the kitchen of the Boston home of Alice and George Hastings.

ROSALIE O'KEEFE: Remember, keep your eyes and your ears and your thoughts to yourself. The Hastings aren't paying you a dollar a week for your opinions. You'll start here in the kitchen, helping out Kathleen. Mind what she says.

KATHLEEN MAGUIRE: I'll only say it the one time.

NORA O'KEEFE: Yes ma'am. (*She watches in awe as Kathleen drops potatoes in a pot of water.*) How many people live here?

KATHLEEN MAGUIRE: There'll be just the four for dinner tonight—the Mr. and Mrs., her sister, and little Alice.

NORA O'KEEFE: All that food for four people—and one a child!?

ROSALIE O'KEEFE (*gently*): Things are different here in America. Everyone has plenty here, even us.

KATHLEEN MAGUIRE: That's right. There's no famine here. No potato blight.

NORA O'KEEFE: If there's so much here, why don't they send some over to Ireland where it's needed?

KATHLEEN MAGUIRE: Hush, now. No talk like that in this house. We're here, aren't we? We'll go to bed with full bellies tonight, won't we? And tomorrow and tomorrow after that?

NORA O'KEEFE: How can I eat my fill and then turn around and go to sleep when I know that my own poor family is lucky to be sharing *one* potato for dinner?

ROSALIE O'KEEFE: You don't think about it, Nora. You work hard, and you save so we can bring them all over to America. You're the oldest girl. It's right that you're here. You must do your duty.

KATHLEEN MAGUIRE: Such serious talk, and in my kitchen! I can see that it's time to bring out the fancy cakes.

NORA O'KEEFE: Fancy cakes! I must be dreaming!

KATHLEEN MAGUIRE: Now, listen, miss. You'll get a fancy cake from me now and again, but if I ever catch you taking one from a tray that's going out to the dining room—you'll be out on the streets. I don't care if you're Rosalie's niece or not.

NORA O'KEEFE: Just *looking* at a fancy cake is enough to satisfy me.

Scene 3: Three months later, in the Hastings' dining room. Nora is alone in the room, dusting. She sees a five-dollar bill lying under a chair. She reaches to pick it up and then thinks better of it.

NORA O'KEEFE: Sure, and it's a test they've put out for me. What should I do? Should I leave it lay? Or should I put it on the table where they're sure to see it? What if Mrs. Hastings, or the Mr., walks in, with me holding the money? They'll think I was about to slip it into my pocket. But what if the wind blows it under the china hutch? They'll think I've stolen it, sure.

(She paces up and down the room, trying to decide what to do.)

I can't lose my job. I've nowhere else to go. What will happen to Aunt Rosy if they think I'm a thief? They'll toss her out, too. They might even call the police. They might send us straight back to Ireland. No, they would never do that. They'd send us straight off to jail. Think of the shame when Mother and Da find out. What should I do? What should I do?

ALICE HASTINGS *(calling from the hall)*: And remember, Kathleen, my father is coming for dinner tonight so that means no onions in any of the food. Don't forget!

(Nora suddenly decides. She grabs the money and places it on a silver tray, underneath a sugar bowl, where it's clearly visible and won't blow away. When Alice Hastings walks into the room a second later, Nora is on the other side of the room, dusting the chairs. Alice immediately looks under the chair. She seems almost pleased to see that the money is gone.)

NORA O'KEEFE: Morning, ma'am.

ALICE HASTINGS *(jumping and looking startled)*: Nora! You startled me!

NORA O'KEEFE: I'm sorry, ma'am.

ALICE HASTINGS: My father's coming for dinner tonight, so I want to make sure everything sparkles and shines.

NORA O'KEEFE: Shall I polish the silver, ma'am?

(Alice turns toward the silver tray and sees the money. Trying to conceal her surprise, she takes it and folds it into the sleeve of her dress.)

ALICE HASTINGS: You're either a very good girl, Nora, or a very smart one.

NORA O'KEEFE: Both, I hope, ma'am.

ALICE HASTINGS: Do you like it here, Nora? Are you happy with us?

NORA O'KEEFE: Yes, ma'am. You've been very kind to take me in.

ALICE HASTINGS: There are a great many girls who would do almost anything to be in your position. I don't suppose you realize how lucky you are to be here. You could be working long, hard hours in a factory.

NORA O'KEEFE: I can't believe it sometimes, ma'am. To be warm and well fed, to live in a such a beautiful house . . . I hope you're not disappointed in my work.

ALICE HASTINGS: Yes, do polish the silver, Nora. Make sure it sparkles and shines. Don't disappoint me.

ACT 3

Scene: 1865. Inside the parlor of a Boston boardinghouse. The house is in good shape but needs some minor repairs.

ROSALIE O'KEEFE: Imagine! It's been 18 years since I've seen my brother Michael and your mother, Bridget. You weren't even born yet when I left Ireland.

BRIDGET O'KEEFE: Do you think they'll be pleased with the house? Maybe we should have waited till they got here to buy it.

ROSALIE O'KEEFE: They'll be very pleased. Listen! Is that the carriage? (*They both rush to the window to look out.*) There's Mary. Can that be Joseph? Look how tall he is! Where's Michael? Where's my little brother?

BRIDGET O'KEEFE: Da's gone, I know it. He's caught the fever on the crossing. He's gone.

(*Nora, Mary, and Joseph enter the room.*)

NORA O'KEEFE: Here we are! My goodness, such long faces!

BRIDGET O'KEEFE: Where's Da?

JOSEPH O'KEEFE: I thought you said we were going to a boardinghouse. Where are all the other boarders? Working?

MARY O'KEEFE: Bridget, my great big girl, if you don't come over here and give your mother a hug, I don't know what I'll do.

ROSALIE O'KEEFE: Get it over with, Mary. Just tell it quick.

NORA O'KEEFE (*smiling at Joseph*): What's the matter? Don't you enjoy a bit of room?

BRIDGET O'KEEFE (*tearfully*): How can you just stand there talking, when poor Da is—is—

NORA O'KEEFE: Coming in the next carriage with the trunks? Have you forgotten how your own father is? Would he leave his family's possessions in the charge of anyone but himself?

ROSALIE O'KEEFE (*sounding relieved*): When we didn't see him, we thought he'd caught the fever coming over and died.

MARY O'KEEFE: Three did. We had to bury them at sea. Those poor families. Imagine leaving Ireland a married woman and arriving in America a widow.

JOSEPH O'KEEFE: Are we the only boarders here? And why is that? What's wrong with the place that everyone else shuns it?

NORA O'KEEFE: Look around you, Joseph. Do you see anything that looks so terrible?

JOSEPH O'KEEFE: Now that you mention it, the stairs look a little rickety—

MICHAEL O'KEEFE (*shouting from offstage*): Here, you! Watch that trunk! Bring it on! Bring it on!

(*When he enters, everyone clusters around him.*)

BRIDGET O'KEEFE: We thought you were dead!

ROSALIE O'KEEFE: Ah, Michael, it's so good to see you!

MICHAEL O'KEEFE: Rosy, and my little Bridget. I never thought I'd see you again!

NORA O'KEEFE: Everyone, come and sit down. Have some tea and cakes.

JOSEPH O'KEEFE: Tea *and* cakes?

ROSALIE O'KEEFE (*laughing*): He sounds just like you, Nora, when you first came over.

(*Everyone sits down.*)

NORA O'KEEFE: What do you think of the boardinghouse? Do you think you'll feel comfortable here?

MARY O'KEEFE (*looking around*): It's grand. I don't think I'll ever want to leave it.

MICHAEL O'KEEFE: We'll be wanting to get our own house, once we've put some money by. (*Nora, Bridget, and Rosalie look at each other and start to laugh.*) What's so funny, I'd like to know?

ROSALIE O'KEEFE: This *is* a boardinghouse—

BRIDGET O'KEEFE: It's *our* boardinghouse—

NORA O'KEEFE: We're not guests. We *own* it.

ROSALIE O'KEEFE: We've six rooms set aside for boarders, and the rest are for us.

BRIDGET O'KEEFE: And room for a garden in the back, Da.

NORA O'KEEFE: It's a sweet house. It only wants a little bit of fixing up.

MICHAEL O'KEEFE (*winking*): So you brought us over here to put us to work, is that it, my girls?

NORA O'KEEFE (*a little anxiously*): You do like the house, don't you?

MARY O'KEEFE: It's a grand, proper house. Just look how the wood floor shines.

JOSEPH O'KEEFE: The stairs look a little rickety—

MICHAEL O'KEEFE: Roll up your sleeves, my boy, we've got a little work to do.

(*Michael and Joseph start wandering through the house, inspecting it.*)

NORA O'KEEFE: It's all right, isn't it, Ma? Us getting the house?

MARY O'KEEFE: It's more than all right, Nora. You and Bridget and Rosalie have given us a home. We're all together again—that's the only thing that matters. We're all together again under one strong roof.

Background on
IRISH AMERICANS

Introduced to Spain in the late 1500s, the potato was not immediately considered as a source of food. By the end of the 1600s, however, the Irish people and economy depended on the potato as a food staple and a major crop. That ended in 1845 when blight struck. The fungus *Phytophthora infestans* caused the Great Famine in Ireland, which lasted for about ten years. Farmers were unable to pay their English landlords rent, and many were evicted so their sod houses could be torn down and the land opened up for grazing. About one million Irish people died during the famine. Millions more immigrated, primarily to the United States. On the night before someone's departure to the United States, an "American wake" would be held with music and storytelling; family and friends didn't expect to see them again. Most of the immigrants were young people, and many young women went to work in service in private homes or in factories. Arriving immigrants often faced discrimination in the form of "No Irish Need Apply" signs that some employers posted.

Most of the Irish immigrants fleeing the potato famine arrived in New York City. From 1855 until 1890, immigrants landed at Castle Garden, an island south of Manhattan. They were able to find information at Castle Garden about jobs and shelter and exchange their currency. In 1890, due to the large number of immigrants flooding into New York, the federal government opened Ellis Island in New York Harbor. Annie Moore, a 15-year-old girl from County Cork in Ireland, was the first person to arrive at Ellis Island.

In addition to the potato famine, rural overpopulation and a lack of jobs caused many Irish to emigrate. In 1841, Ireland had a population of 8,000,000. By 1900, the population had dropped to half of that figure. During the Great Depression, immigration laws put a limit on the number of immigrants allowed into the United States. The rate of Irish immigration slowed to about 13,000 a year. It remained low until the 1980s when Ireland was hit by unemployment.

According to the current U.S. census, about 39 million Americans claim Irish ancestry; since 1821, more than 4,700,000 Irish have immigrated to this country. In fact, more Irish live outside Ireland today than in the country.

BIBLIOGRAPHY

Conlon-McKenna, Marita. *Wildflower Girl*. New York: Puffin Books, 1994.

Denenberg, Barry. *So Far from Home: The Diary of Mary Driscoll, an Irish Mill Girl*. New York: Scholastic, 1997.

Hoobler, Dorothy and Thomas. *The Irish American Family Album*. New York: Oxford University Press, 1995.

Watts, J.F. *Irish Americans*. New York: Chelsea House Publishers, 1988.

ACTIVITIES

SPEAK OUT!

Emigrant or Immigrant? • Explain that Nora was both an *emigrant* and an *immigrant*. She emigrated from Ireland. She immigrated to the United States. To clarify students' understanding of the two words, ask them to look up the words in the dictionary. Have students pay special attention to the origins of the words, as well as their definitions. Talk about how knowing the origins can help them remember the words' definitions.

An Ocean Away • Discuss Nora's situation with the class. On the one hand, she was lucky to leave Ireland and the famine behind; on the other hand, she was separated from her family and friends. Encourage students to put themselves in Nora's place and think about what they would miss the most about their own homes. How would they feel about being separated from their families and friends and going to strange, new places? What would they do to manage their homesickness?

WRITE NOW!

Where in the World Are We From? • Create a bulletin board that shows where in the world students' relatives came from. Hang a world map on the bulletin board. Then let students tack drawings or photos of themselves on the countries where their relatives originally lived. They should also write captions giving any facts that they know, such as relatives' names, the places where they lived, and the dates that they moved. Students can also attach yarn leader lines to show where the relatives settled in the United States.

THE IRISH IN AMERICA

Devote wall space in your classroom to an Irish American Hall of Fame. Students can write brief biographies or compile family albums of famous Irish Americans—or the not-so-famous such as grandparents. Allow time for students to "induct" their nominees into the hall of fame. You may also want to suggest that students discover the Irish influences in your community.

GET DOWN TO THE FACTS!

Mr. Potato in Peru • The potato is thought to be native to the Andes, and South American farmers probably began growing it more than 1,800 years ago. Ask students to find out more about how the potato was introduced to other parts of the world. Encourage creativity in the ways in which they present their findings. For instance, students may make world maps with flow lines to show the spread of the potato as a crop. Artistic students may also want to create a short comic-book history of the potato. Computer-literate students may want to design a Web page. Students who enjoy cooking may collect a variety of potato recipes from different world cuisines.

HUNGER AND MIGRATION

Remind students that the potato famine in Ireland had a direct impact on the United States population. Talk about what famine is and the effects it can have on individuals, families, and countries and regions. Direct pairs of students to study major famines in the past. What impact did the famines have on populations in the famine-stricken countries and in other countries? How does famine affect immigration? Can they link the decrease and increase in the population figures of two or more countries and attribute the connection to famine?

The West Wind Carries My Thoughts

CAST OF CHARACTERS

(in order of appearance)

Roy Ng: Guide at Angel Island Immigration Station

Tina Chu: Sixth-grade girl visiting Angel Island Immigration Station

Paul Chu: Tina's father

Maxine Chu: Tina's mother

Yung Lin: Gold prospector; Paul's great-grandfather

Beau Saunders: Gold prospector

Louis Fabre: Storekeeper

Tom Lo: Merchant

Sammy Lo (Yik Sem): Tom Lo's "paper son"; Maxine's grandfather

Chin Li Chu: Paul's grandmother

Lois Wong: Chinese immigrant

Inspector Barnett: Immigration official

Wei Shee: Chinese immigrant

PROLOGUE

Scene: Present day, Angel Island Immigration Station in San Francisco.

ROY NG: Welcome to the Angel Island Immigration Station. My name is Roy Ng. Is this your first visit to Angel Island?

TINA CHU: Yes, but my great-grandmother Chin Li was here for a long time. We want to find the poem she wrote. Sammy Lo, my great-grandfather on my other side, was here, too, but we don't know if he wrote a poem or not. He never said.

ROY NG: Most of the poems are unsigned. Some of them have been destroyed over the years. It may not be possible to find your great-grandmother's poem, but let's see what we can do.

TINA CHU: I know the poem. She used to recite it to my father. He wrote it down in Chinese and in English. I'll know it when I see it.

ROY NG: Well, let's get started on our tour then. I'll just tell you about Angel Island as we walk. From the years 1910 through 1940, over one million Asian immigrants came here to Angel Island. Some stayed days. Some stayed weeks or months. Some even stayed here for years. Sadly, some were sent back.

PAUL CHU: What happened before then? My great-granddad came here during the Gold Rush. My dad says he thinks maybe around the 1850s or 1860s. Something like that.

ROY NG: Really, until the year 1882, Chinese could come to the United States, provided they could scrape together the money for their passage. The Gold Rush brought the first big wave of Chinese to the United States. A family might mortgage their land to buy a ticket for a son to come to America. Many hoped to stay here for a few years, just long enough to make some money, and then return to China. Most stayed, though.

PAUL CHU: Yung Lin, my great-great-granddad, stayed. He came here searching for *Gum Shan*, the Gold Mountain, and he found it. He only went back to China to marry and bring his wife back with him. They were able to get back into the United States without any trouble. But Chin Li—my grandmother— when my granddad brought her from China, she was held here for six months.

MAXINE CHU: I still think it's so strange that your grandmother and my grand– father were here at Angel Island at the same time.

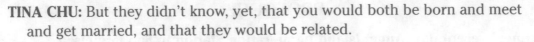

TINA CHU: But they didn't know, yet, that you would both be born and meet and get married, and that they would be related.

MAXINE CHU: No, that's true. My grandfather was having a hard enough time trying to keep his new name and his new history straight. He was a paper son. A merchant sponsored him.

TINA CHU: Do you want to hear their stories, Mr. Ng?

ACT 1: In Search of Gum Shan

Scene 1: 1858, at a gold-mining claim a few miles outside of Marysville, California.

YUNG LIN: How long have you worked the claim?

BEAU SAUNDERS: Long enough to know that either I'm no prospector or I'm just plain unlucky.

YUNG LIN: The price seems high.

BEAU SAUNDERS (*quickly*): Because I haven't overworked it. There's gold there, I'm sure of it. As sure as I am that I'm not cut out for this kind of work. I just want to make enough money to get back home to Indiana. This is *Gum Shan*, all right. This is Gold Mountain.

YUNG LIN: How about the other miners in the area? Are there many?

BEAU SAUNDERS: Everybody pretty much keeps to themselves. You might get into trouble in Marysville if you walk by the wrong man. You might get your pigtail there pulled.

YUNG LIN: By law in China we must wear our hair like this.

BEAU SAUNDERS: Some people might tell you that this isn't China.

YUNG LIN: Like you, we're going back home one day. So we keep our "pigtails."

BEAU: Tell you what—you pay me for this claim, and you can keep your pigtail *and* all the gold you find.

Scene 2: 1859, in the Marysville general store.

LOUIS FABRE: The word is you're finding a lot of gold on Beau Saunders's old claim.

YUNG LIN: A little gold.

LOUIS FABRE: The word is you're using some kind of new mining techniques out there. Water wheels or some such thing.

YUNG LIN: Old mining techniques in China. May I have five pounds of sugar, please?

LOUIS FABRE: If you have as much gold dust as I hear you have, you can have anything in this store.

YUNG LIN: Just five pounds of sugar, please.

LOUIS FABRE (*laughing and shaking his head*): You Celestials, you sure play your hands close to your chests. Is that all I'm going to get out of you? A little gold, old mining techniques, five pounds sugar. Don't you get lonely, being so far from home? What about your family? How long has it been since you've seen your relatives? You might even have a wife and children waiting back in China for you to come back a rich man. It must be hard, but I guess life's got to be pretty poor back there.

YUNG LIN: How much for the sugar?

LOUIS FABRE: I hope for your sake that you're married. I don't think I've ever seen a Chinese woman in this country. If you plan on staying here, I don't know how you'll ever find yourself a Chinese woman for a wife.

YUNG LIN: The best place to find a Chinese woman is in China. How much for the sugar?

LOUIS FABRE: Say—did you see the new dime novels that just came in? Best way in the world to enlarge your English vocabulary. I don't imagine you get much company out there on your claim.

ACT 2: "Paper Sons" and Real Wives

Scene 1: 1915, on board the steamship *Liberty* headed for San Francisco. Tom Lo and his "paper son" Sammy Lo are standing at the ship's rail. Tom is testing Sammy.

TOM LO: What is your name?

SAMMY LO: Sammy Lo.

TOM LO: How many outside doors does your house in China have?

SAMMY LO: Two outside doors—one small and one large.

TOM LO: Who lives in the second house in your row?

SAMMY LO: Second house in my row? (*thinking*) Leon Gai.

TOM LO: You can't stop and think. You have to *know*. Tell me about Leon Gai's wife.

SAMMY LO: Her name is Gong Shee. She has bound feet.

TOM LO: Do they have any children?

SAMMY LO: Two sons.

TOM LO: Who lives in the third house in the first row in your village?

SAMMY LO: Third house, first row . . . is . . . Yi Chun Yau.

TOM LO: No. There is no Yi Chun Yau in my village.

SAMMY LO (*miserably*): I forgot. He lives in my village.

TOM LO: You have to forget who you are and where you came from. Remember only this: you are my son, born in my village. You're a student. Once you convince the *luk yi* that you are my son and they let you into America, then you can go back to being who you really are.

SAMMY LO: I don't like lying.

TOM LO: Neither do I, but what choice do we have? Chinese Exclusion Act says no Chinese workers can come into America. Merchants are okay. Students are okay. I've lived in America for 25 years. I'm a merchant. Before, if I try to visit my family in China and come back to the U.S., *luk yi* looks at me and says, "Maybe you are a merchant and maybe you aren't." There was no guarantee that they would let me back in. Then the earthquake hits. All the birth records in San Francisco go up in smoke. Now is my chance. I apply for citizenship, say I was born in U.S., in San Francisco. What can they say? They have to believe me. Now it's your chance. I'm an American citizen now. I can bring my family back from China. I have no real son. You have no real father in America. So you be my "paper son." Okay?

SAMMY (*nodding*): Okay. Lin Shee lives in the third house, first row. She is a widow, no children, bound feet.

Scene 2: 1915, five months later, on Angel Island. Chin Li Chu is watching her friend Lois Wong knit.

CHIN LI CHU: How many sweaters have you made since you've been here?

LOIS WONG: Five. This makes six.

CHIN LI CHU: Will you teach me to knit? I'm going crazy, just sitting here, waiting.

LOIS WONG: Don't be silly. Neither of us is going to be here long enough for me to teach you to knit.

CHIN LI CHU: How long have you been here?

LOIS WONG: Eight weeks.

CHIN LI CHU: I've been here six weeks. I don't think either of us is going anywhere soon, do you?

LOIS WONG: You must be optimistic. I'll tell you what. If you write a poem for me, I'll teach you how to knit.

(They hear shouting from the men's section downstairs. Both women rush over to the windows to look out.)

CHIN LI CHU: Look! They've released some of the men! Do you recognize anyone?

SAMMY LO *(calling from offstage)*: So long, Angel Island! So long, *luk yi*—green-clothes men!

LOIS WONG: I recognize that voice—it's Yik Sem from my village. He was a farmer there. I wonder what he'll be here.

CHIN LI CHU: Why do you think they finally let him go? What's the right thing to say, to make the *luk yi* let you go?

LOIS WONG: Aii, I wish I knew. Here, come sit by me, and I'll show you how to cast on. Wrap the yarn around your fingers like this—

(The door opens, and Inspector Barnett enters the room. He looks around.)

INSPECTOR BARNETT: Wei Shee! Wei Shee! *(He rubs his eyes as if he is crying.)*

WEI SHEE: No! No! You cannot send me back! My husband is here! I belong here with him! *(She tries to back away from Inspector Barnett, but he takes her by the arm.)*

INSPECTOR BARNETT: Chin Li Chu! Chin Li Chu!

CHIN LI CHU *(burying her face in her hands)*: Oh, no!

INSPECTOR BARNETT: Chin Li! Chin Li! *Sai gaai*! It's your lucky day!

LOIS WONG *(hugging Chin Li)*: *Sai gaai!* Good luck! You're free!

INSPECTOR BARNETT: Lois Wong! Lois Wong! *Sai gaai* to you, too!

EPILOGUE

Scene: Present day, Angel Island Immigration Station. Roy Ng and the Chu family are walking in the hall leading to what was once the basketball court at Angel Island. The walls are lined with handwritten poems in Chinese.

ROY NG: The wood is softer here than in the other rooms. It was easier to carve the poems here. But some people wrote in ink—one man even wrote poetry on the underside of his canvas cot! Soon it was hard to find space on the walls; the poems were everywhere, people expressing themselves.

MAXINE CHU: It must have been so hard, waiting here. As beautiful and as sad as the poems are, I still can't imagine what it must have been like. Waiting here, not knowing if you would see your family again—in China or in the United States.

PAUL CHU: Paper sons waiting for paper permission to enter the country. Sammy Lo remained Sammy Lo. He was afraid to take back his name once he was admitted into the U.S.

TINA CHU: Look! I've found it! I've found Chin Li's poem! "The west wind carries my thoughts to you." That's it, isn't it? That's the first line!

(Everyone hurries over to Tina. They touch the wall carefully.)

PAUL CHU: That's it. (*softly*) Chin Li was here.

Background on
CHINESE AMERICANS

Poverty and famine, political instability, and news of the California Gold Rush of 1848 boosted Chinese immigration to the United States. More than 20 million people died during the Taiping Rebellion from 1850 to 1864, in which peasants rose up against landlords. Between the years of 1820 and 1847, about 1,000 Chinese arrived in the United States. By 1880, the Chinese population topped 100,000, most of whom were settled in the West. The largest number of Chinese emigrated from the Guangdong (Kwangtung) Province in southeastern China. Most of the immigrants were males, hoping to work for a few years in America and return to China as rich men. Those who were married left their wives and children behind; Chinese custom demanded that women care for their husbands' ancestors.

At first, the Chinese were welcomed in this country. They worked long hours for little pay. Chinese prospectors also bought out gold claims that were considered "played out." Using mining techniques unfamiliar in this country, many were able to make the claims profitable—but some went bust. The building of the transcontinental railroad provided job opportunities for a host of first-generation immigrants. More than 15,000 Chinese worked for the Central Pacific Railroad, which was laying track from the west to the east to meet the Union Pacific Railroad and link the country. After 1869, when the transcontinental railroad was completed, the railroad workers found themselves unemployed and competing for jobs. Then, in 1873, a depression hit the United States, and the economic situation worsened. Resentment against Chinese immigrants was stirred to such an extent that anti-Chinese riots broke out in several cities. Congress passed the Chinese Exclusion Act of 1882 which halted the immigration of Chinese workers.

Although the earlier Burlingame Treaty of 1868 had allowed for the free migration of Chinese, the treaty had not allowed them to become naturalized citizens. The only way to become an American citizen was to be born in the United States. Indirectly, the earthquake that struck San Francisco in 1906 had an impact on Chinese immigration. Fires destroyed birth records. Chinese men could claim to have been born in the United States and receive citizenship. They could then bring their wives and families to join them in America. In some cases, fathers brought in "paper sons"—young Chinese men unrelated to them.

In 1943, with China as a wartime ally, the United States finally repealed the Chinese Exclusion Act.

BIBLIOGRAPHY

Fraser, Mary Ann. *Ten Mile Day and the Building of the Transcontinental Railroad*. New York: Henry Holt, 1996.

Hom, Marion K. *Songs of Gold Mountain: Cantonese Rhymes from San Francisco Chinatown*. Berkeley: University of California Press, 1992.

Lai, Him Mark, Genny Lim, and Judy Yung. *Island: Poetry and History of Chinese Immigrants on Angel Island, 1910–1940*. Seattle: University of Washington Press, 1991.

Takai, Ronald. *Journey to Gold Mountain: The Chinese in 19th-Century America*. New York: Chelsea House Publishers, 1994.

ACTIVITIES

SPEAK OUT!

The Power of the Word • Write the word *immigrant* on the board. Ask students what the first words that come into their minds are. Discuss their responses.

What Would Life Be Like? • Pose the following question to students: *What would American life be like today if Chinese immigrants hadn't come to this country?* Share the example of Lue Gim Gong, who developed an orange that would produce fruit year-round in Florida. Encourage students to bring in and discuss biographies of Chinese Americans who have made contributions to American lives.

WRITE NOW!

60 Days on the Sea • Many of the early Chinese immigrants to the United States came from the Guangdong (Kwangtung) Province. They took ships from China to California, and the trip took about 60 days. Most passengers took their own food and bedding in addition to their clothing and other personal items. Have students locate Guangdong Province and San Francisco on a world map and then plan a sea route between the two places. If they were immigrating to America, what would they take with them to start a new life? Ask students to determine the distance of the route and figure about how many miles per day a ship would travel if a trip lasted about 60 days. Allow time for them to compare routes and what they would take.

Saving Angel Island • In the early 1970s, when the buildings at Angel Island were scheduled for demolition, a park ranger discovered poems written by the Chinese immigrants. Direct students to investigate the history of Angel Island, from its beginnings to its designation as a National Historic Landmark. Encourage them to write poems describing its history. If the book *Island: Poetry and History of Chinese Immigrants on Angel Island, 1910–1940,* listed in the bibliography above, is available in your community, obtain a copy and let each student choose a poem. Hold a seminar on Angel Island for other classes in your school, sharing its history and reading aloud its poetry.

GET DOWN TO THE FACTS!

Panning for Gold and Working on the Railroad • Chinese laborers made an impact in the gold fields of California and on the Central Pacific Railroad. Challenge students to research the California Gold Rush of 1848 or the completion of the transcontinental railroad in 1869 to learn about the contribution of other immigrant groups to each event. Encourage them to seek folk songs, poetry, short stories by writers such as Bret Harte, or nonfiction by Mark Twain written about the Gold Rush or the railroad. Compare and contrast these works with passages about the same time periods from *China Men* by Maxine Hong Kingston.

Closing the Door on the Chinese • Numerous laws were enacted to keep Chinese immigrants from enjoying the full benefits of American life. These included California state laws such as the Foreign Miner's Tax in 1853, the Immigrant Tax in 1855, and the Act Relating to Fishing in the Waters of This State in 1880, and San Francisco city ordinances such as the Queue Ordinance in 1876 and the Laundry Ordinance in 1879. The federal government enacted the Burlingame Treaty in 1868, which encouraged Chinese migration but prohibited their naturalization, and the Chinese Exclusion Act of 1882, which shut the door on Chinese immigrants. Guide students in tracking down laws and ordinances that directly affected Chinese immigrants. Compile their findings and discuss the effects of each law and ordinance. Expand your class's research to include court cases such as the *Yick Wo* decision made by the Supreme Court in 1886, *Ling Sing v. Washburn*, and the *People v. Hall*.

A Pack Full of Dreams

CAST OF CHARACTERS
(in order of appearance)

Wedad Habib: Peddler

Joseph Azar: Supplier for the peddlers

Feris Habib: Wedad's husband; a peddler

Tuma Habib: Feris's brother; a peddler

Salwa Habib: Feris's and Tuma's sister; a peddler

Abboud Khouri: a peddler

Michael Azar: Supplier for the peddlers; Joseph's brother

Kamila Azar: Joseph's and Michael's mother

Grace Malina: Nebraska farmer

ACT 1

Scene: 1909 in a small house in Fort Wayne, Indiana, which is home to the Habib and Azar families.

WEDAD HABIB: I worry about my English.

JOSEPH AZAR: Don't worry, don't worry. All you have to do is open your pack. The pots and pans will speak for themselves. Your customers know what they need. Don't worry, they'll tell you.

FERIS HABIB: Your English is much better than mine was when I started. (*laughs*) I remember once, a miner in West Virginia wanted a little something for his son. Yes, I thought, something for the sun—and I brought out a sun bonnet! He wouldn't buy anything from me after that.

TUMA HABIB: Worry about the dogs you're going to meet, Wedad. Have you seen my scar where the black dog in Ohio bit—

JOSEPH AZAR: We've seen it, we've seen it!

SALWA HABIB: I once met a peddler on the road who told me that he'd been chased and bitten by a *chicken*! Can you believe that? A *chicken*!

ABBOUD KHOURI: No. I believe you, Salwa, but I don't believe him.

MICHAEL AZAR (*sighing*): You know, sometimes I miss being on the road. I never got bitten. I never really had any trouble. Sure, some people were suspicious—some people are always going to be suspicious, but it became a challenge for me to try to win them over. Those were the people who I really took pride in selling something to.

JOSEPH AZAR: Go back on the road if you want to. Me, I'm happy right here, filling up peddlers' packs, hearing their stories. That's close enough for me, close enough.

KAMILA AZAR: I'm lucky to have my family here with me, all of us under one roof, working together.

WEDAD HABIB: I wonder if I'll ever get to see my family again. Mount Lebanon seems so far away . . . I don't know where my brother Yusef is . . .

JOSEPH AZAR: We'll find him, don't worry, don't worry. I've put the word out to all the other peddlers. They'll spread the word. If he's out west, it may take a while, but we'll find him, don't worry.

FERIS HABIB: At least he's not being forced to serve in the Ottoman army. It's enough that the Ottomans' tax our villages and take all our money—they shouldn't have all our men. The Turks don't speak for Mount Lebanon. They never have.

SALWA HABIB: Wedad, be sure to let the women touch the olive wood, the mother of pearl, the lace, the embroidery. Let them handle the things for the kitchen, the knives, the spoons. Let them fall in love a little with the things. Let them talk, too. The farms are so scattered, they don't get many visitors. It will help your English, too, talking with them, listening to them talk.

MICHAEL AZAR (*nodding*): Most people will trust you more than they'll trust a man who's carrying a pack.

ABBOUD KHOURI (*sighing and patting his stomach*): They'll probably ask you to have supper with them, too. We men, we just have to be content with the food that Kamila has packed for us—

KAMILA AZAR (*mimicking Abboud*): Ooohh, Kamila, nobody bakes pita the way that you do. Add a few more rounds to my pile, eh? Ooohh, Kamila, two more pieces of baklava, please. I'll be away for so long. Have pity on me.

ABBOUD KHOURI (*defensively*): It's hard work, peddling. A man gets hungry. Carrying a pack on his back—a hundred pounds easily—carrying a suitcase or two also, trudging down those red dog roads in West Virginia—

TUMA HABIB: What you need, Abboud, is a wagon with a fine team of horses.

ABBOUD KHOURI: My thoughts exactly! A fine, shiny wagon with a pair of white horses. The rest of you save your money to open your own stores. Not me, I'm going to buy a wagon! Think of all the things I can carry with me!

TUMA HABIB: A man riding in a wagon doesn't have to worry about getting bitten by a dog.

FERIS HABIB: Or tired feet and an aching back.

(*Wedad begins to look alarmed.*)

SALWA HABIB: Don't listen to them, Wedad. You'll be fine. Always take a few minutes to rest under the shade of a tree, Wedad. Never pass by a stream without stopping. Fill your water bottle. Bathe your face. Soak your feet.

ABBOUD KHOURI: A man with a wagon and a fine team of horses earns some respect in this country.

KAMILA AZAR: Remember, Wedad, to set out the sweets for your customers too—and the bread. Remember who likes the baklava and who likes the bird's nest. I'll bake whatever they like.

WEDAD HABIB (*murmuring*): So much to remember . . .

ACT 2

Scene: Two months later. At a farmhouse in Nebraska. Wedad knocks on the door. Grace comes around the side of the house.

GRACE MALINA: Yes? (*She sees Wedad's pack.*) Ah, a peddler. I warn you—we have not had a good year.

WEDAD HABIB (*nodding in sympathy*): The wheat should be higher. The clouds should bring rain.

GRACE MALINA: I would very glad to *see* a cloud float by—just one. (*Wedad takes off her pack, glad for a rest, and stretches a little.*) Well, the least I can do is offer you a glass of water and a chair. Come inside. (*They enter the tidy kitchen of the farmhouse.*) Here—sit here at the table.

WEDAD HABIB: I spoke to your husband, Mr. Malina, when I was last by here. He said that maybe in a few months you would be needing some white thread.

GRACE MALINE: There are many things that we need, but things cost money.

WEDAD HABIB: Maybe not so much money. In a month, you may have to throw away a pair of pants or a dress that could have been saved with some white thread today.

GRACE MALINA: Ah, but your pack is full of so many things. The thread I need is probably packed at the very bottom. You'll need to unpack so many pretty things to get to it.

WEDAD HABIB: Not so many things, but it's true, they are all very pretty things.

GRACE MALINA: You see—you haven't even opened up your pack, and you've made me so curious about what you've got inside it. Unfortunately, I can't afford to be curious.

WEDAD HABIB: I understand. (*She stands up and begins to shoulder her pack.*) Perhaps when I'm here next fall.

GRACE MALINA: Oh, don't go so soon! You look like you could use a rest—I've got a piece of vinegar pie left over if you're hungry. Antonin says he's tired of vinegar pie. My children say they're tired of it, too. To tell you the truth, I'm a little tired of vinegar pie, too. I hate to see it go to waste—unless you really have to go?

WEDAD HABIB: I've never had vinegar pie. I should try it at least once.

GRACE MALINA: Good! How about some coffee? You really can't have vinegar pie without coffee.

WEDAD HABIB: If it's no trouble . . .

GRACE MALINA: No trouble. (*She puts on the coffeepot and gets out the pie. Wedad stands up and walks around the kitchen, stretching her arms occasionally. She stops in front of a drawing of a landscape. Grace notices Wedad's interest.*) Bohemia—the most beautiful place in the world.

WEDAD HABIB: You might not say that if you'd ever visited Mount Lebanon.

GRACE MALINA: Well, I've never actually visited Bohemia, either. My grandmother drew that. She was born there. She moved here with her family when she was 14.

WEDAD HABIB: She came with her family? Her whole family?

GRACE MALINA: Yes, her parents, three brothers, two sisters. And you? Are you here alone?

WEDAD HABIB: No, but my mother and father are still in Mount Lebanon. My husband is here, and most of his family.

GRACE MALINA: You must miss your parents very much.

WEDAD HABIB (*nodding*): They don't want to leave. They say they're too old to move.

GRACE MALINA: Will you and your husband go back, or will you stay here?

WEDAD HABIB: We'll stay here. It's too crowded there. Too many people and not enough land for everyone. You were born here in America?

GRACE MALINA: Fifteen miles down the road in Milligan. Have you been here long?

WEDAD HABIB: Less than a year, but sometimes it seems like a very long time.

GRACE MALINA: You came in through Ellis Island? (*Wedad nods.*) What was that like?

WEDAD HABIB: Big . . . crowded . . . noisy . . . but all different languages, like everyone in the world was there. It was strange. (*shaking her head*) I don't have the words to describe what it was like.

GRACE MALINA: And now, when you're not traveling, where do you live?

WEDAD HABIB: In Fort Wayne, Indiana, with my husband's family and the Azars and Abboud, another peddler. The Azars are suppliers for a lot of peddlers. The railroad brings the supplies to the Azars, and Michael and Joseph give the supplies to us, and out we go.

GRACE MALINA: Do you know—I've never even ridden on the railroad? I would love to, though. I would love to travel—but with a farm like this, you can't. This is why my family came here to America—for the land—160 acres of it. We're lucky, I know. In Bohemia, maybe you could have a little bit of land to grow vegetables for your family, but only the rich could have this much land. Here, all you have to do is promise to live and work the land for at least five years. Five years is not so long.

WEDAD HABIB: There's so much land here, and . . . it's all so . . . different. Abboud tells us about the mining camps in West Virginia. My brother Yusef has been in Arizona and California and tells us about the desert and the ocean. My husband, Feris, has traveled along the Mississippi River all the way down to New Orleans. And here, in Nebraska, not so many trees and no mountains. Not like Mount Lebanon at all. That's good, though, I would miss my home too much if America was too much like Mount Lebanon. I mean, I would miss where I grew up . . . this is my home now.

GRACE MALINA: Ah, but you travel so much. How much time do you spend in one place?

WEDAD HABIB: We won't always be traveling around so much. In a few years, Feris and I will have enough money to open our own store. But maybe not in Fort Wayne, maybe someplace where there are a few hills and a river.

GRACE MALINA: I envy you—getting to travel—seeing new places and meeting new people. Sometimes, I don't see anybody but Antonin and my children for weeks—I love them, but a little company now and then is nice. Like you.

WEDAD HABIB: You've been very kind to me. The pie was delicious. From the name, I wasn't sure whether I would like it. (*She starts rummaging in her pack.*)

GRACE MALINA: Oh, no! I really, really can't afford to buy anything from you—I'm so sorry—I wish I could.

WEDAD HABIB (*placing a spool of white thread on the table*): A trade for the coffee and the pie. I'll be back in the fall, and then in the spring. Maybe you can buy something then.

GRACE MALINA: I don't even know your name! You see—I have so little company that I've completely forgotten most of my manners. I'm Grace Malina. I'm very pleased to meet you.

WEDAD HABIB: My name is Wedad Habib. I'm very pleased to meet you, too. (*She shoulders her pack.*)

GRACE MALINA: You'll come back in the fall—you promise? Who knows—we might get some rain yet. You might be able to sell me something beautiful—something that I *want*, instead of something that I need.

WEDAD HABIB: My pack will be full of the most beautiful things the next time I see you. Good-bye. Thank you for the vinegar pie.

GRACE MALINA: Thank you for the thread—and the company. Be careful, Wedad. (*Wedad walks out the door. Grace stands at the door for a long time, watching and then she calls out.*) Good-bye! Good-bye! I'll see you in the fall. (*whispering*) Such a long time to wait for a friend to visit with.

Background on
ARAB AMERICANS AND CZECH AMERICANS

The CEDARS OF LEBANON

Mount Lebanon, or the Lebanon Mountains in present-day Lebanon, lie between the Mediterranean Sea and the Beka'a Valley. The steep, rugged mountains offered protection against invaders, but arable land, although fertile, was sparse and had to be terraced. After the Ottoman Turks conquered what is now Lebanon in 1516, the isolation of the Mount Lebanon area and its fairly strong government run by a prince and feudal lords gave the region some autonomy. This autonomy drew immigrants from other parts of the Ottoman Empire, and the population of Mount Lebanon increased substantially. Tension among religious groups arose. The Ottomans also began drafting young men from Mount Lebanon into the Turkish army. Then, in 1876, merchants and artisans from Mount Lebanon first visited the United States for the Philadelphia Centennial Exposition, where they displayed arts and crafts. Their enthusiastic descriptions of "Amrika" sparked interest in immigration to the United States. Like many other immigrant groups, Arab families used precious savings or mortgaged their land to pay the passage to America for their sons and daughters, who, in turn, sent money back home or paid for their parents and other relatives to join them in America. The Lebanese—both men and women—preferred to work by themselves as peddlers rather than undertaking factory or mining labor. Traveling around the country and meeting different people helped the Lebanese immigrants learn English quickly and become familiar with American customs and culture. After peddling for a few years, many were able to become suppliers or buy their own stores.

Until January 1, 1993, the provinces of Bohemia, Moravia, and Slovakia made up the republic of Czechoslovakia. Then the republic split into the Czech

Republic and Slovakia. Bohemia is in the Czech Republic in the west. Mountains surround its central area of plains and hills. The city of Prague is located in Bohemia and once served as the capital of the province. Both Czechs and Slovaks lived in the three provinces, but the majority of people in Bohemia were Czechs. In 1526, the Austrian Hapsburg empire took control of the three provinces, and they became part of Austria-Hungary. In March of 1848, rebellion against the Hapsburg empire swept through Bohemia. The rebellion failed, and many Bohemians began immigrating to the United States. Economic rather than political reasons continued to bring Czechs to America. Whole families migrated, and the moves were considered permanent. Large Czech communities grew up in the Midwest and Texas where land was plentiful.

BIBLIOGRAPHY

Cather, Willa. *My Ántonia*. Boston: Houghton Mifflin, 1918. (for older readers)

Harik, Elsa Marston. *The Lebanese in America*. Minneapolis: Lerner Publication Company, 1987.

Naff, Alixa. *The Arab Americans*. New York: Chelsea House Publishers, 1988.

Saxon-Ford, Stephanie. *The Czech Americans*. New York: Chelsea House Publishers, 1989.

Shefelman, Janice. *A Peddler's Dream*. Boston: Houghton Mifflin, 1992.

ACTIVITIES

SPEAK OUT!

Career Choices • Like Wedad, many emigrants from Mount Lebanon became peddlers and then opened their own stores. J.M. Haggar and Mansour Farah both achieved fame by establishing clothing factories, while some Lebanese immigrants opened silk kimono factories. After World War I, a large number of Muslim immigrants from Mount Lebanon worked in the auto industry in Michigan. Bohemian immigrants were prominent in the cigar-making industry in New York City. Like Grace Malina's family, many Czechs took advantage of the Homestead Act and began farming their 160 acres of land. Discuss with students which career choices customarily open to American immigrants they would have been interested in—farming, mining, working in a factory or starting one, peddling, or shopkeeping—and why.

A Pack Full of Dreams • A peddler's pack could contain many useful things that a rural family far away from a store might need, such as pots and pans, tools, utensils, clothing, and beautiful, uniquely Lebanese items such as objects carved from olive wood and silk fabric. Ask students to use their imaginations in making their own peddler's packs. Emphasize the balance of necessary or practical items with beautiful objects. They may use their own backpacks filled with items, create a drawing or collage showing the contents of packs, or design a Web page highlighting the wares of a modern-day peddler. Set aside time for peddlers to present their wares to other students.

WRITE NOW!

Chickpeas or Garbanzo Beans? • Introduce students to food associated with Lebanon such as hummus, pita bread, and baklava. If possible, bring in samples of each for your class to try. Then have students find recipes for these and other Lebanese dishes. Ask them to increase the ingredients to produce enough of the dishes for the entire class and to rewrite the recipes using the new proportions.

An American Hall of Fame • Ray Kroc, the founder of McDonald's, was of Czech descent. The heart surgeon Dr. Michael DeBakey and his sister Professor Lois DeBakey are of Lebanese descent. Which Czech American and Lebanese American would students nominate to an American Hall of Fame? Start an American Hall of Fame scrapbook in a three-ring binder with dividers for sections such as Politics and Government, Science, Arts, Business, and so on. Encourage each student to add an Arab American and a Czech American to the notebook. They should list each person's accomplishments, supply a biography, give their reasons for honoring him or her, and include any other relevant or fascinating information. Rather than following a set format for each page, urge students to present their material in a variety of ways.

GET DOWN TO THE FACTS!

Location, Location • Both Lebanon and Bohemia contain mountainous regions. Divide the class into groups of four or more students. Charge them with the task of drawing physical maps of present-day Lebanon and Czechoslovakia. Their maps should show and label mountains, valleys, rivers, and seas, and also icons representing the natural resources of the countries. Remind them to include complete legends with their maps. Then let students decide where Wedad and her family lived on Mount Lebanon and where Grace Malina's family lived in Bohemia, and locate and label those places on their maps.

Escaping from the Ottomans and the Hapsburgs • Explain to students that when Wedad immigrated to the United States, the country of Lebanon didn't yet exist, and that when Grace Malina's grandmother came here, Czechoslovakia wasn't then a country. Have the same groups from the ***Location, Location*** activity research the histories of Lebanon and Czechoslovakia. After collecting their data, tell them to focus on the period from World I to the present in both countries. At which periods would they expect an increase in emigration from Lebanon and Czechoslovakia? Which factors do they think would most influence someone's decision to emigrate? Discuss each group's conclusions.

A Fair Day's Wages...

CAST OF CHARACTERS
(in order of appearance)

First Narrator

Second Narrator

Max Halpern: Young Jewish man born in Russia

Joseph Halpern: Max's father

Ruth Halpern: Max's mother

Golda Leavitt: Joseph's sister

Emma Halpern: Max's younger sister

Inspector Harmon: Ellis Island health inspector

Hannah Strauss: Emma's coworker at the garment factory

Eli Singer: Foreman at the garment factory

Jacob Meyer: Union leader

Workers 1–4

Strikebreakers 1–4: Speaking and nonspeaking roles

Scabs 1–4: Nonspeaking roles

ACT 1

Scene: 1905, a *shtetl*—village—in the Jewish Pale of Settlement, Russia.

FIRST NARRATOR: The empress Catherine the Great ruled Russia from 1762 to 1796. She greatly increased the size of Russia by invading Poland and seizing control of much of its land and people, including the largest Jewish community in the world at the time. This portion of Russia came to be known as the Pale of Settlement. The government said that all Jewish people in Russia had to live in the Pale.

SECOND NARRATOR: Life in Russia continued to get harder for Jewish people. Jewish males, sometimes as young as 12, were forced to serve in the Russian army. Their army service could be as long as 25 years. With the approval of Russian leaders, a series of pogroms were carried out against the Jewish people. The Russian word *pogromit* means "to destroy" and that's just what other Russians did to Jewish shtetls, towns, and cities. Jews were murdered and injured and their property was destroyed or stolen. They had no protection.

MAX HALPERN: I'm not going! I'm not going to serve in the army of a country that's ready to kill me!

JOSEPH HALPERN (*flatly*): If you don't do as they say, and go into the army, they'll kill you.

MAX HALPERN: I don't care! Russia can't fight me and my people and then expect me to pick up a gun and defend it against Japan! It's not my war! It's not my fight!

RUTH HALPERN (*gently*): Max, don't make it so hard on yourself, or us. They will come and get you, one way or the other.

GOLDA LEAVITT: I can't believe what you're saying. Either of you. This is your son. You're about to lose him.

RUTH HALPERN: What can we do?

JOSEPH HALPERN: It's your fault that he's talking so, Golda. You come here and you spread such stories—

GOLDA LEAVITT: They're not stories, Joseph. I saw these things with my own eyes. I saw my friends and neighbors being killed and hurt. I saw such horrible things that you can't even imagine. Didn't I come to you without anything but the clothes on my back? They took everything. They destroyed *everything*.

JOSEPH HALPERN: Then how did you manage to survive?

GOLDA LEAVITT: How many times do I have to tell you? The people from the hospital found me. They wrapped me in bandages so they could take me to the hospital and keep me safe there. I don't know how many other people they managed to save that way.

EMMA HALPERN: America.

JOSEPH HALPERN (*startled*): What?

RUTH HALPERN (*quickly*): She didn't say anything.

MAX HALPERN: Yes, she did. She said "America."

RUTH HALPERN: She didn't mean it. She doesn't know what she's saying.

EMMA HALPERN: Yes, I do.

JOSEPH HALPERN (*turning angrily to Golda*): I told you not to say anything in front of the children.

GOLDA LEAVITT: She has a right to know that her aunt is going to America.

JOSEPH HALPERN: You need a passport to leave. The government won't give you a passport. It won't give any of us a passport. Don't talk such foolishness in my house.

MAX HALPERN (*boldly*): I'm going with Aunt Golda to America.

JOSEPH HALPERN: Do you see, Golda? Do you see how you upset everyone with your talk? It's one thing to risk your own life, but you're putting all of us in danger. If they catch you, they'll make all of us pay.

MAX HALPERN: They already make us pay—every day, by telling us where we have to live and what we can do and not do. And even that isn't enough. Then they come sweeping into homes and cut our throats. I won't live like that—

JOSEPH HALPERN: That's right, you won't. Keep talking like that, and you won't, believe me.

RUTH HALPERN (*suddenly*): Max is right. He doesn't have a chance here. Neither does Emma.

JOSEPH HALPERN: No. No more talk.

RUTH HALPERN: We can get work, Joseph. Hasn't my cousin Solomon begged you to come to New York? Hasn't he offered to pay our passage if we would come to work in his factory?

GOLDA LEAVITT: All we have to do is get to Hamburg. He'll have the tickets waiting for us.

JOSEPH HALPERN: And then we'll be obligated to him for the rest of our lives. No.

MAX HALPERN: I'm going. I don't care what I have to do. I'll work 20 hours a day cutting out dresses or sewing buttons on shirts. I don't care.

RUTH HALPERN: The Bernsteins made it to Hamburg. I know how they did it. I know who to contact to take us across the border.

GOLDA LEAVITT: We won't be able to take much with us, but—

JOSEPH HALPERN: Go, then! All of you! Go to America! See if I care!

ACT 2

Scene: Four months later on Ellis Island in New York Harbor.

FIRST NARRATOR: The Halperns and Golda Leavitt left the shtetl in the middle of the night. They each carried a pack with clothes, a few small belongings, and some food. Two Gentile men—men who were not Jewish—helped smuggle them across the border into Germany. Then everyone boarded a train for Hamburg, a city on the coast, where they would catch a ship to America.

SECOND NARRATOR: Ruth's cousin Solomon had promised that he would pay for their passage and that tickets would be waiting for them in Hamburg. There were no tickets. Other Jewish emigrants were waiting for promised tickets, too. Many had already paid travel agents, who swindled them out of their money. Their tickets never arrived. Fortunately, Solomon kept his promise, and the tickets soon arrived. He needed workers in his garment factory—especially workers who owed him something.

FIRST NARRATOR: Before the Halperns and Golda Leavitt could board the steamship to America, they had to pass a physical examination. Anyone with an eye disease called trachoma, lice, or tuberculosis wasn't allowed to board. Fortunately, everyone passed the exam.

SECOND NARRATOR: The trip from Hamburg to New York took ten days. Food was scarce. People were sick. They were crammed into close quarters with each other. The air and water were bad. The Halperns and Golda spent as much time on deck as they could, hoping to spot land and talking to other emigrants about what lie ahead. Emma was the first one to spot the Statue of Liberty in New York Harbor. Soon, they landed at Ellis Island.

INSPECTOR HARMON: Two lines! Men over there! Women and kids over there! Step lively! I don't care if you can't understand me—just follow everybody else.

JOSEPH HALPERN (*unwilling to be separated from his family*): No! We were examined in Germany!

INSPECTOR HARMON: Well, you're in America now. You're going to get an American examination.

MAX HALPERN (*tugging his father's arm*): Come on, Papa. We'll see them soon.

INSPECTOR HARMON: In or out—make up your mind, old man. Into America— or back to wherever you came from. That's right! Step lively!

(*Joseph reluctantly moves with Max to the men's line. He stands on his toes so he can see the progress of his wife, his daughter, and his sister. Max hears someone speaking Yiddish, a language spoken by many Jewish people from eastern Europe, and turns to find out who's talking.*)

JOSEPH HALPERN: No! No, no, no! Don't touch her hair! Don't cut my daughter's hair! Max! Max! Look what they're doing to your sister. Stop them! We were checked already in Germany! Oh, her hair! Her beautiful hair!

MAX HALPERN: Papa, ssshh! Her hair will grow back. Better that Emma's hair is short and she's in America than she's sent back to Russia with her long hair. (*shifts his father around so he can't see Emma or the others*) Here, meet Saul Rabinowitz. His brother owns a pushcart. He says his brother goes up and down Hester Street and in one day can make one dollar selling cloth and shoes—

JOSEPH HALPERN: How much is one dollar?

MAX HALPERN: I don't know, but it sounds like a lot. What's Solomon going to pay us?

JOSEPH HALPERN: He's paid our way over here, and you're asking how much he's going to *pay* us?

MAX HALPERN: It's a fair question. He's getting five workers, isn't he? Five good workers.

JOSEPH HALPERN: Five workers who don't know anything about the garment business.

MAX HALPERN (*shrugs*): Cutting and sewing clothes, how hard can that be?

JOSEPH HALPERN: I hope Ruth can recognize Solomon. It's been so long since they've seen each other. Maybe he's given up on us. Maybe he's come down here every day for days, looking for us, and we weren't here . . .

MAX HALPERN: Papa, relax, this is America. Nobody in America has to worry about anything.

JOSEPH HALPERN: That's because I'm here now. I'll worry enough for everybody.

INSPECTOR HARMON: Next! Take off your coat and shirt, old man. Cough for the doc. (*He pushes Joseph toward an open door.*) Got another one for you, doc. Sure looks tubercular to me.

JOSEPH HALPERN (*anxiously to Max*): Keep your eyes on your mama. Don't lose her! Don't let anything happen to them!

MAX HALPERN: Papa, don't worry!

(*Max tries to look calm as his father disappears into the examination room. He looks around wildly when he realizes that he can't see any of his family.*)

MAX HALPERN: What if something happens? What if they send me back? What if all of us don't make it in? What if we're separated? We may never see each other again. *Never.* We shouldn't have come. We should never have left Russia. This is all my fault.

ACT 3

Scene: 1907, at Solomon's garment factory on the Lower East Side of New York City.

FIRST NARRATOR: The Halperns and Golda Leavitt passed their health examinations and were allowed to leave Ellis Island. With Cousin Solomon's help, they found an apartment in a tenement building on the Lower East Side of New York City. Joseph, Max, and Emma worked in Solomon's garment factory. Ruth and Golda worked at home, sewing garments.

SECOND NARRATOR: Garment factories were called "sweatshops" because the workers worked from 12 to 14 to 16 hours a day for very little pay. They were often locked inside the buildings, and the work areas had little ventilation. Factory rules were strict, and the foremen enforced them.

HANNAH STRAUSS (*whispering to Emma who sits at a sewing machine next to hers*): Did you hear? Sophie got fired. She didn't finish enough sleeves.

EMMA HALPERN: It's so hot in here today. How can they expect us to work fast when it's so hot?

HANNAH STRAUSS: It's always hot in here. Did you—

EMMA HALPERN: Ssshh. Here comes Eli the Terrible.

ELI SINGER: Clara needs collars, Emma Halpern! Right now! Your workbox is empty, but it appears that your mind is full. You know what happens to workers who don't produce. Fill your mind with *that*.

HANNAH STRAUSS (*waiting until Eli is across the room*): You look terrible. Did you eat anything for lunch?

EMMA HALPERN: I didn't have time. Besides, I wasn't hungry.

HANNAH STRAUSS: Max keeps looking at you like he's worried.

EMMA HALPERN (*irritably*): He's probably looking at you, wondering why you keep bothering me so I can't work—

HANNAH STRAUSS: What? You can't talk and work at the same time? Since when? You must be sick.

EMMA HALPERN: I'm not sick! I can't be sick. I have to work so we can buy the *shifskart*, the steamship ticket, for my cousin—

HANNAH STRAUSS: Tell Solomon. Have him send your cousin a ticket.

EMMA HALPERN: My cousin can't work here. His hands were hurt . . . he was attacked in a pogrom.

HANNAH STRAUSS: Here, take it. Take this collar. Put it in your workbox.

EMMA HALPERN: No . . . I can't. I—

(*Emma faints and falls to the floor. Hannah hurries over to her friend. Max runs across the room. Seeing this, Eli comes out of his office.*)

HANNAH STRAUSS: Someone get me a wet cloth! We need to bathe her face.

MAX HALPERN(*kneels down beside his sister*): Emma! Emma! Can you hear me? Wake up!

ELI SINGER: Everybody back to work! Now! That means you, Hannah Strauss. You, too, Max Halpern. Or do you want to be fired like your sister here?

MAX HALPERN: Fired? For what? For being worked to death? For not being paid enough money? For not being able to breathe clean air?

HANNAH STRAUSS (*gives Max a warning look*): Look—she's coming around. She's fine, Mr. Singer. You'll see. Just give her a few minutes, and she'll be back at her machine. She'll catch up.

ELI SINGER: I've got 20 girls lined up at the door, begging for her job. Twenty healthy girls. Twenty hardworking, quiet girls. When she comes to, send her home. I don't want her in my factory.

MAX HALPERN (*stands and faces Eli*): Then you don't want me, either.

ELI SINGER: No, I don't. But Solomon does. You owe him quite a bit of money. Someone in your family has to pay. Now, honor your debt and get back to work.

EMMA HALPERN (*opens her eyes and looks confused*): What happened? Let me up! I have to get back to work! Let me up!

MAX HALPERN: No, no. Relax, Emma. You fainted. You're going home.

EMMA HALPERN: No! I have to work! I have to—

HANNAH STRAUSS: So you'll work at home with your mother and your aunt. I'll come by and visit you.

EMMA HALPERN: He fired me? Why? I'm fine!

MAX HALPERN: Hannah's right. You'll work at home with Mama and Golda.

EMMA HALPERN (*wildly*): I can't go home! What will I tell them? We have to bring Uncle Leo over! They'll kill him!

HANNAH STRAUSS (*feels Emma's forehead, then whispers to Max*): Her forehead is like fire. (*to Emma*) Can you stand up? If we help, do you think you can stand up?

MAX HALPERN: I'll carry her home if I have to.

(*They help Emma to her feet and start walking to the door.*)

HANNAH STRAUSS: No, I'll take her home. You can't afford to lose your job, too. Solomon will take everything you have for his debt.

MAX HALPERN: What about you?

HANNAH STRAUSS: There's a union shop over on Stanton Street. Nine hours of work for the same pay as here. I have a friend who works there. She'll help me get on there.

MAX HALPERN: A union shop? They're all revolutionaries—socialists and anarchists.

HANNAH STRAUSS (*laughs*): Max. "A fair wage for a fair day's work." Is that so revolutionary? Or do you like that better—(*she points her chin at a sign on the wall*)—"If you don't come in on Sunday, then don't come in on Monday"?

MAX HALPERN: I don't want anything to happen to you.

HANNAH STRAUSS: Anything good—or just anything bad?

MAX HALPERN (*looks embarrassed*) : You know what I mean.

ELI SINGER (*shouts from across the room*): MAX! BACK TO WORK! NOW! HANNAH—

HANNAH STRAUSS (*shouts back*): I QUIT!

ACT 4

Scene 1: 1909, inside a tenement building on Essex Street on the Lower East Side.

FIRST NARRATOR: Emma slowly recovered from her illness. She worked at home—a small, crowded apartment in a tenement building on Essex Street. Alongside her mother and her aunt, she still sat for long hours over a sewing machine. Sometimes Ruth sent Emma to help Joseph when he rented a push-cart for the day. They went to wholesale stores on Orchard Street early in the morning and bought goods such as clothes and shoes and then sold them from the pushcart.

SECOND NARRATOR: Max remained at Solomon's garment factory. The conditions there remained harsh—children and adults worked long and hard for little pay in unsanitary and unsafe conditions. He continued to see Hannah, who worked in a factory represented by the ILGWU (the International Ladies' Garment Workers Union). In 1909, the ILGWU called for a general strike to fight for better wages and working conditions. More than 20,000 workers, both union and nonunion, in more than 500 factories walked off their jobs in support of the strike. Max Halpern was one of those workers.

JOSEPH HALPERN: You had no right to do this! No right! Do you have any idea what will become of us? Do you know what Solomon will do to us? Do you?

MAX HALPERN: Papa, look at what he's already done to us—

JOSEPH HALPERN: Oh, yes, such a bad man! Giving us the tickets to come here and start new lives. Giving you and your sister jobs in his factory, and your mother and Golda work to do here at home. Getting us this apartment. Oh, yes, shame on Solomon!

MAX HALPERN: We've paid him back, Papa. We've more than paid him back. He'll never let us forget what he's done for us—

JOSEPH HALPERN: And we shouldn't forget, either!

MAX HALPERN: What about Emma? He's responsible for almost killing her.

JOSEPH HALPERN: This is not you talking! This is that Hannah Strauss talking. She's putting words into your mouth, crazy ideas into your head!

MAX HALPERN: Papa, I'm not going to cross the picket line and go back to work. I've joined the union.

JOSEPH HALPERN: Then I'll have to take your place. I honor my debts.

MAX HALPERN: I honor my fellow workers. I honor my family, who deserves more than this.

JOSEPH HALPERN: You know nothing about honor. You disgrace me. You disgrace your family. You are not my son. I want you to leave this house.

Scene 2: A few days later, in front of Solomon's garment factory.

JACOB MEYER: Okay, men, pay attention! We march in twos in front of the factory door. Watch out for *shtarkers*. They'll try to break our lines and get the scabs in. Be careful. Those goons won't be polite about it. They won't hesitate to hurt us. Watch out for each other. Ready?

MAX HALPERN (*to his partner, Worker 1*): How can you tell who's a shtarke and who's not?

WORKER 1 (*laughs*): Not to worry, you'll know. He'll be the one who knocks you off the sidewalk and hopes the police wagon runs you over.

MAX HALPERN: Listen, my father's coming here today . . . as a scab. I couldn't stop him. I don't want him to go inside that factory, but I'm going to make sure he gets in safely.

WORKER 1: Not to worry, we'll watch out for him.

WORKER 2: Here they come!

WORKER 3: Shtarke and scabs!

JACOB MEYER: Hold fast!

WORKER 4: Where are the police? Why aren't they here to protect us?

WORKER 1: Don't worry, if they were here, they wouldn't be here to protect us.

WORKER 2: When you see the police—that's the time to start worrying.

JACOB MEYER: March, men!

WORKER 3: Hey!

(The strikebreakers wade into the workers, pushing them out of the way. The scabs try to make their way to the factory door.)

MAX HALPERN: Papa!

JOSEPH HALPERN: I don't know you! Get away from me!

MAX HALPERN: Papa, don't go in! Please! Think about what you're doing!

JOSEPH HALPERN: Get out of my way!

MAX HALPERN: Let me help you get inside then.

STRIKEBREAKER 1 *(takes Max's arm)*: You heard him! Get away!

(He pushes Max against the side of the building. Max falls heavily.)

JOSEPH HALPERN *(turns on Strikebreaker 1)*: Leave him alone! He's done nothing to you!

STRIKEBREAKER 1 *(tries to shove Joseph inside the building)*: Shut up and get inside, scab!

(Worker 1 grabs Strikebreaker 1's arms so Joseph can get away.)

WORKER 1: Get inside, quick! Don't worry, you'll be safe!

(The other strikebreakers advance on Max, who is still dazed and lying on the ground.)

JOSEPH HALPERN *(grabs a board lying near the door and waves it at the advancing strikebreakers)*: Get back! All of you! Get away from my son!

MAX HALPERN *(rises slowly to his feet)*: Papa, you have to get inside! Quickly!

JOSEPH HALPERN: No. I'm staying out here, with you.

WORKER 2: Look! Here come workers from the other factories! Reinforcements!

WORKER 3: Shtarker—where are you going? Why are you running away so fast?

WORKER 4: I didn't think they could run so fast.

JACOB MEYER: Ready? March in twos!

JOSEPH HALPERN *(extends his hand to Max and then hesitates)*: It would be an honor to march with you, but . . . maybe you already have a partner . . .

MAX HALPERN *(takes his father's hand)*: No, I need a partner.

Background on
RUSSIAN JEWISH AMERICANS

Between the 15th and 16th centuries, Poland had become the safest place in Europe for Jewish people. Jews had been forced out of England, France, and Spain. Hundreds of thousands had been killed during the Spanish Inquisition and in German territories. Poland, alone, adopted the rights of Jews into their legal code. This came to an end in 1772. For the next 23 years, Russia, Prussia, and Austria attacked Poland and seized much of its territory. The largest Jewish community in the world was now under the control of Russia. Because they weren't Slavs or Christians, Russian Jews faced persecution. They were allowed to live only in the Pale of Settlement. Boys as young as 12 were subject to service in the Russian army—sometimes for as long as 25 years. As soldiers, they were forced to attend Christian religious services on Sundays and to eat pork, which is prohibited by Jewish law.

As early as 1648, Cossacks—the cavalry of czar's army—swept into Poland and killed 100,000 Jews. Massacres, or pogroms, such as these continued to occur over the next 250 years. Under Czar Alexander II, restrictions against the Jews loosened somewhat. Some Jewish people were able to live outside the Pale in cities such as Moscow and St. Petersburg. In 1881, the czar was assassinated, and Jews were falsely blamed. Consequently, a series of pogroms were carried out in 1881–1882. Over one third of the Jewish population emigrated; 90 percent of them came to America. Other massive pogroms were carried out in 1903, 1905, and 1919 in response to poor social and economic conditions and the rise of revolutionary movements within Russia.

Russian Jews arriving in the United States entered through the ports of Philadelphia; Boston; Baltimore; and Galveston, Texas. But the greatest number flocked to the port of New York City. Before 1892, all immigrants were processed though Castle Gardens. On January 1, 1892, Ellis Island opened and became the point of entry. American Jews set up organizations such as the Hebrew Immigrant Aid Society (HIAS) to help eastern European Jews entering Ellis Island.

In New York City, the Lower East Side became home to many eastern European Jews. They lived in tenement buildings, often sharing apartments with other families or lodgers. Many, including children, worked in the garment industry, either in sweatshop factories or at home. The hours were long, from daybreak until well after dark, and the pay was low. Conditions in the factories and the tenements were often dangerous and unsanitary. This led to the rise of unions in the garment industry. In 1888, the United Hebrew Trades was organized to protect the rights of Jewish workers. In 1900, the International Ladies' Garment Workers Union (ILGWU) was established. At an ILGWU meeting in New York City in 1909, Clara Lemlich, a young Jewish garment worker, spoke out for a general strike for better wages and working conditions. About 20,000 workers in 500 factories joined the strike. More than 300 employers agreed to the strikers' demands.

BIBLIOGRAPHY

Freedman, Russell. *Immigrant Kids*. New York: E.P. Dutton, 1980.

Hesse, Karen. *Letters from Rifka*. New York: Puffin, 1993.

Lawlor, Veronica. *I Was Dreaming to Come to America: Memories from the Ellis Island Oral History Project*. New York: Viking, 1995.

Meltzer, Milton. *The Jews in America: A Picture Album*. Philadelphia: The Jewish Publication Society, 1974.

Woodruff, Elvira. *The Orphan of Ellis Island*. New York: Scholastic, 1997.

ACTIVITIES

SPEAK OUT!

Say That Again • To give students a sense of what it might have been like to arrive at Ellis Island without knowing English, conduct the following activity. Invite someone to class who speaks a foreign language, preferably one not familiar to any of your students. Ask her or him to present a task to students in that language. You might, for example, suggest the instructions for a game. Encourage the students to try to foster communication by using gestures, diagrams, and any other strategies they think might work. Afterward, discuss the experience with students and your guest speaker. How well did they manage to communicate with each other? What was the most frustrating part of the activity? What was the most rewarding? Ask students to consider the problems faced by the immigrants who didn't speak English and by inspectors who had to deal with many different languages.

Diaspora • The Roman Empire invaded Palestine and conquered Jerusalem in A.D. 70. In A.D. 135, the Romans outlawed Judaism and ordered Palestinian Jews to disperse throughout communities outside of Palestine. This dispersion is called the Diaspora. Discuss the Diaspora with students. Do they think that something like that could ever happen in the United States? Could a group of people— united by religious or political beliefs or because of their race or ethnicity—ever be banished from the United States? If such a Diaspora occurred again elsewhere in the world, should the United States intervene? Urge students to justify their thinking.

WRITE NOW!

Carrying My Home with Me • Like the Halperns and Golda Leavitt, many emigrating Russians left their homes quickly, able only to carry a few of their possessions. Challenge students to imagine themselves in that position. Which possessions would they take with them to their new homes, and why? Have students, at home, set aside the possessions they would like to take, and then try to fit the possessions inside an empty grocery bag. If all the possessions don't fit, they must decide which things to leave behind. How did students feel about having to leave these things behind? Ask them to keep a journal of their process.

Life on Ellis Island • Turn your students into playwrights. Commission them to write plays about Ellis Island. They may focus on one particular person or family, a diverse groups of immigrants, different time periods, or how and why Ellis Island was restored and turned into a national park. Encourage writers to study as many oral histories and reminiscences as they can from the people who passed through Ellis Island to get a feeling for what life was like. You may want to let playwrights collaborate and work together in groups or pairs.

GET DOWN TO THE FACTS!

To Strike or Not to Strike? • Present the following situation to students: "Suppose the cafeteria workers at our school decided to strike. How do you think such a strike would affect you? Would you support the strike if it were over the issue of pay? Would you support the strike if it were over the issue of safety?" After talking about the hypothetical situation, have groups of three or five students research strikes that have occurred in the United States. Each group should select one strike; for example, the football strike in 1982 or the Northwest Airlines pilots' strike in 1998, and research it thoroughly. One group member should be the mediator, and the remaining members should be divided evenly between the two sides involved in the strike. Have groups try to resolve the strikes successfully. The mediator should keep a record of the negotiations. Compare their results with the real settlements.

Jewish Holidays • List the following Jewish holidays on the board: Rosh Hashanah, Yom Kippur, Sukkoth, Sehmini Atzereth, Simchas Torah, Hanukkah, Purim, Pesach (Passover). Have groups of students find out more about each holiday, including the time of the year that it's celebrated, its history, and how it's celebrated today. Display a 12-month calendar, and let groups mark their holidays on it. You also may want to let students invite speakers before the holidays to talk about their importance and to share their family traditions in celebrating the holidays.

The Longest 90 Miles in the World

CAST OF CHARACTERS
(in order of appearance)

Mr. Espinosa: Social studies teacher
Celia Longoria: Student
César Longoria: Celia Longoria's great-grandfather
Andy Salcines: Student
Sandra Jackson: Student
Roberto Cruz: Student
Paulina Salcines: Andy's grandmother
David Haya: Roberto's neighbor; a Miami newspaper reporter

ACT 1: César Longoria's Story

Scene: Present day, a social studies class in Miami, Florida.

MR. ESPINOSA: We have a special guest today. Celia Longoria's great-grandfather, Mr. César Longario, is going to tell us a little something about what Florida was like in the 1930's. Celia, would you like to introduce your great-grandfather?

CELIA: My great-grandfather was born in the Oriente province of Cuba in 1915. When he was 15, he came to Florida to work in a cigar factory. Then he went back to Cuba and met and married my great-grandmother. They had six children. Two of their children, including my grandfather, are still in Cuba. One of their other children lives in Spain. The other three live here in the United States. Um . . . I guess that's all. He can tell you the rest. Please welcome my great-grandfather, César Longoria.

(As Mr. Espinosa and his students clap, César Longoria comes to sit in a chair in front of the classroom.)

CÉSAR: Thank you, thank you. *Muchas gracias, muchas gracias.* I'm very pleased to be here today. I know a lot of your families came from Cuba.

ANDY: My grandmother says she's going back to Cuba. She says it to me every day. Sometimes she says it four or five times every day. I don't know why she wants to go back.

CÉSAR: Have you ever asked her?

ANDY: No. But only because I don't want her to leave here. I want her to stay in the United States with us.

CÉSAR: She means she misses her old life in Cuba. She misses the way things used to be there. For some of us, the United States has become our home. Others are just waiting, living here in exile.

CELIA: What does that mean?

MR. ESPINOSA: "Exile" means someone who is separated from his or her home, either voluntarily or by the government.

SANDRA: Why did you come to the United States, Mr. Longoria?

CÉSAR: To work. The first time, in 1929, was to work in a cigar factory near Tampa, in Ybor City. I was just a kid, a young teenager. I started as a bunchmaker. I would make bunches of tobacco for the cigar rollers. Pretty soon, I became a roller myself. We would work in long rows of tables and chairs.

The best part of the job, besides the money, was getting to listen to the *lector*. We workers would hire lectors to read to us while we worked. We had four different lectors in a day. Some would read from the newspapers, both American and Cuban newspapers. Some would read from novels.

ROBERTO: That's like getting to watch TV while I'm doing my homework.

CÉSAR: Not quite, not quite. Our hands were busy, always busy, while we worked, but our minds weren't always busy. When you do your homework, your mind is busy, right?

ROBERTO: Of course—sure.

MR. ESPINOSA: Mr. Longoria means that he was also getting an education when he listened to the lector. He was learning ideas that he might not have had time to learn otherwise.

CÉSAR: Exactly, exactly. Listening to the *lecturas* was the way I went to school.

SANDRA: Do they still have lectors?

CÉSAR: Not anymore. Not since 1931. The bosses wanted to tell the lectors what to read. Sometimes they didn't like what we wanted the lectors to read. But the bosses didn't pay the lectors—we workers did. Then the bosses said "No more, no more lectors."

ROBERTO: It's a great idea, though!

CÉSAR: I agree, Roberto, I agree. And you should have heard some of the lectors. They were more than readers—they were *actors*. They made us *see* and *hear* what they read.

SANDRA: Why did you go back to Cuba?

CÉSAR: I had saved some money, and I wanted to get married and start my own family. And I did. I met Celia's great-grandmother in 1937.

ANDY: It's hard, though, having part of your family in Cuba and part of them here. My grandmother's sister still lives in Cuba. Everybody else is here, in the United States, but I know my grandmother misses her. Sometimes I tell my grandmother, "She's only 90 miles away, Lina." She just shakes her head and looks sad.

CÉSAR: But, for her, it must seem like the longest 90 miles in the world.

ACT 2: Paulina Salcines's Story

Scene: Later that day, at Andy Salcines's house.

ANDY: Tell me a story, Lina. Tell me a story about Cuba.

PAULINA: What's gotten into you? You never want to hear me talk about Cuba.

ANDY: Because you want to be there, instead of being happy here with us.

PAULINA: I want all of us to be able to return to Cuba. I want Cuba to be the way it was when I was your age.

ANDY: But I'm happy here. I want you to be happy here, too.

PAULINA: It's not that simple, Andy. Your grandfather and I lost everything when we came here. Everything—you understand? Your grandfather and I lost our work—work we loved doing—work we studied hard to be able to do. We lost our property—the house I grew up in, the things that my father and my mother had given to me. I lost my sister—

ANDY: But she could come here! Aunt Gracy could come here and live with us!

PAULINA: She says she's too old to move now. For a long time, she didn't want to leave. Then she couldn't leave. She was a teacher. Castro needed teachers.

ANDY: Why did you leave then?

PAULINA: Oh, I don't know. I don't know if you're old enough to understand—

ANDY: But I already know. Dad's told me what it was like coming over here. He remembers living in Cuba and then leaving.

PAULINA: Your father thought we were leaving for a little while—he thought we were going on a vacation. He didn't know. Then the government men came and made a list of everything that was in our house, and they sealed up the house, and we couldn't take anything out of it. We were only allowed to carry three changes of clothing with us.

ANDY: But why didn't Aunt Gracy leave with you?

PAULINA: She believed that Castro would change Cuba for the better. She thought the government before Castro was terrible.

ANDY: Then why did you want to leave?

PAULINA: Because we saw what was happening. Things might have been bad before, but they were getting worse and worse. I couldn't practice law the way I wanted to. I was a judge, but it wasn't up to me anymore to show what the law was. Your grandfather was a lawyer too. He tried to represent some of the people who were having their property and money taken by the government—

ANDY: He got into trouble for that, didn't he?

PAULINA: Yes, he did—he almost got put into prison.

ANDY: But you could be lawyers here, too.

PAULINA: We had to take an exam here to practice law. We had to study American law and really get to know English. We didn't have any money—we had to get work so we could eat and pay rent. Your father even had to work. There was no time for anything else.

ANDY: But you don't have to work now, Lina. Mom and Dad have good jobs. You could study now.

PAULINA: But I'm going back to Cuba one day, Andy. What do I need with an American law degree?

ANDY: Dad says "*no tengo regreso*—there's no going back."

PAULINA: Your father is a very smart man, but he doesn't always know what he's talking about.

ANDY: Lina, tell me a happy story about Cuba.

PAULINA: What about the story of Gracy's and my *quinceañeras*? We're twins, you know, so our parents had two 15-year-old girls to throw a big party for. Usually, a girl asks 15 girls to her *quinceañera*, and all the girls wear the same thing—very fancy. Of course, we're twins so we had to have 30 girls! You should have seen it! It was the best *quinceañera* that Havana had ever seen! People talked about it for years and years. Now, nobody in Cuba has *quinceañeras*.

ANDY: They do here, Lina. That proves it! The United States is better than Cuba ever was!

PAULINA: Except that Cuba has something that this country doesn't—my sister Graciela.

ACT 3: David Haya's Story

Scene: The next day, at the newspaper offices of *El Nuevo Herald*.

DAVID: So, Roberto, you want to see how a newspaper works?

ROBERTO: Were you a newspaper reporter in Cuba?

DAVID: Not exactly. I wrote about some of the things I saw and heard . . . that would be like a news story here. I wrote some of my opinions down . . . that would be like an editorial here. I would pass it around to people I knew I could trust . . . but even then, I never signed my name to any of my writing.

ROBERTO: You know what? You should interview César Longoria. He came over here a really long time ago. He was telling us all about working in a cigar factory and how they used to hire people to read to them. He's Celia Longoria's great-grandfather. He's pretty old. None of my great-grandparents are alive. Are yours?

DAVID: No, but my dad used to tell me about *his* great-grandfather, Arturo. Arturo was born in West Africa. When he was a teenager, he got captured and sold to the Spanish. They took him to Cuba to work on the sugar plantations.

ROBERTO: I love sugarcane. Just after it's cut, it's so good and sweet.

DAVID: It's hard work growing sugarcane, and then harvesting it. My Dad said that he never saw Arturo use sugar or any kind of sweetener in his coffee or anything. He couldn't stand the taste after having to be around it all his life.

ROBERTO: He must have missed his family, being taken from Africa like that. Didn't he ever want to go back and find them?

DAVID: Cuba didn't outlaw slavery until 1880 . . . and then all the slaves had to work another six years until they were free. By then Arturo was an old man. He didn't have much money . . . and he had his own family to take care of.

ROBERTO: Do you miss living in Cuba?

DAVID: Sometimes I do.

ROBERTO: Do you think you'll ever go back?

DAVID: No . . . it was too hard getting here. I never want to go back.

ROBERTO: What happened? How did you get here?

DAVID: I was a *balsero*.

ROBERTO: You came over on a raft? You floated over?

DAVID (*nodding*): In 1994 . . . it had gotten very bad in Cuba . . . the Soviet Union collapsed so we weren't getting any more aid from them . . . food was very scarce . . . people were out of work. Then one day Castro says that he wouldn't try to stop anybody who tried to leave Cuba by the sea . . . you should have seen us all, trying to float away from Cuba. Some people just had little rafts they'd knocked together with a few boards and some Styrofoam. The waves just tore them apart.

ROBERTO: You made it though.

DAVID: Barely . . . we were luckier than most . . . we actually had a little boat . . . a fishing boat . . . but it's hard to say no to people . . . so we had 12 people in that little boat. Eight of us made it to the United States.

ROBERTO: Only eight?

DAVID: We started out okay . . . you know, everybody was paddling, leaving Cuba behind, crying and laughing at the same time . . . relieved and scared . . . happy and sad. It was like a parade at first, a big boat parade, a big make-your-own boat parade. Florida is not so far away, we kept telling one another . . . only 90 miles . . . that's nothing . . . a day or two at the most. We didn't have much room, we didn't think we'd be on the sea for that long, so we didn't take much food . . . we didn't *have* much food . . . or water. We wanted to take the things that were important to us . . . things that we couldn't replace.

ROBERTO: What did you take?

DAVID: Pictures and letters . . . some of my writing. I ended up losing almost everything, though. The sea was so rough and there were so many people on our boat . . . it was a very old boat, too . . . that it just came apart. Those of us who could swim tried to keep the others afloat . . . but we were all so tired and hungry and the waves just kept coming . . . some just said "I've had enough" and slipped away. We thought we heard a boat . . . very far away . . . but it was too hard to see us down in the water. And there we were, so thirsty in the hot sun . . . surrounded by all that water . . .

ROBERTO: You're here, though, you made it.

DAVID: *Sí.* On the third day . . . maybe it was the fourth, I don't know . . . a helicopter flew over us . . . they radioed a U.S. Coast Guard ship and they came and picked us up.

ROBERTO: And then you go this job and moved next door to us?

DAVID: Something like that . . . you know, Roberto, I think you'd make a pretty good reporter yourself. Maybe you should interview Mr. Longoria. You might be surprised how many different stories about coming to America there are here in Little Havana.

ROBERTO: You really think I'd make a good reporter?

DAVID: You just interviewed me, didn't you?

ROBERTO (*sounding surprised*): Yeah, I guess I did.

Background on
CUBAN AMERICANS

Some of the first Cuban immigrants were merchants who set up import-export businesses in the port cities of New York and Philadelphia. Then, in the late 1860s and 1870s, many Cuban cigar manufacturers built factories in this country, which were sources of jobs for Cuban immigrants. At one time, Key West had 45 cigar factories, and a ferry service ran between Havana and Key West. While some immigrants remained in the United States, others returned to Cuba.

Other Cubans came to the United States for political reasons. Over the years, Cuba rebelled against Spanish domination. For instance, during the Ten Years' War (1868-1878), thousands of Cubans sought refuge here, primarily settling in the cities of New York, Philadelphia, New Orleans, Boston, and Key West. The United States stepped in in 1898, declaring war against Spain (the Spanish-American War). In 1902, Cuba finally achieved its independence. The new Cuban constitution gave this country the right to intervene in Cuba's affairs to keep the government stable. In 1934, the United States gave up this right but gained a naval base at Guantánamo Bay.

In 1933, Fulgencio Batista spearheaded a revolt to take over the Cuban government. After being elected president and then retiring, Batista overthrew the government again in 1952. He suspended the constitution. Immigration to the United States grew steadily during his regime. In 1958, Fidel Castro and the Fidelistas overthrew Batista. At first, because of Batista's excesses, the change in government was welcomed. Soon, however, Castro led Cuba into communism and the country became a close ally of the Soviet Union.

Wealthy Cubans had their property confiscated. Many of these people, known as the "golden exiles," fled Cuba for the United States. From 1959 until flights between the countries were stopped in 1962, more than 200,000 Cubans entered the United States. After that, until 1965, about 50,000 Cubans flew to third countries, often Spain or Mexico, and then boarded flights to this country.

Castro then decreed in 1965 that Cubans who had relatives living in America could depart on boats from the port of Camarioca. The response was tremendous; people rushed to Camarioca to board often flimsy boats, and many died attempting the 90-mile crossing to Florida. Consequently, Cuba and America began "Freedom Flights" between Varadero, Cuba, and Miami, which carried 300,000 Cubans. These flights were suspended by Castro in 1973, and few Cubans were allowed to leave the country.

In 1978, Cuban Americans were invited to return to their native country for one-week visits with relatives. The visits made many Cubans eager to immigrate to this country. Two years later, in 1980, a group made their way into the Peruvian embassy in Havana and asked for political asylum. After they were allowed to leave Cuba, more than 10,000 people petitioned the embassy for exit visas. To save face, Castro declared that anyone who wanted to go to the United States could leave from the port of Mariel. In just five months, more than 125,000 Cubans left Mariel. Castro also sent thousands of Cubans who were considered undesirables with the "Marielitos." In response, the United States began holding all Marielitos to determine whether they were criminals or not.

Flights between the two countries resumed in 1988, but Cubans who couldn't afford the fare or get visas attempted to cross the sea to Key West. Many of these *balseros*—rafters—lost their lives. When the Soviet Union collapsed in 1991, Cuba lost its economic aid. Food shortages and high unemployment resulted. Three years later, in 1994, Castro said that anyone who wanted to leave Cuba by sea was free to do so. Another surge of *balseros* took to the sea. Because so many lost their lives, Cuba and the United States agreed that all *balseros* heading for the United States would be returned to Cuba.

More than one million Cubans entered the United States between 1960 and 1995 —about 10 percent of the island's population. Not since the influx of Irish immigrants in the 1800s has so high a percentage of a country's people come to America.

BIBLIOGRAPHY

Ada, Alma Flor. *Under the Royal Palms: A Childhood in Cuba.* New York: Atheneum, 1998.

Bogomolny, Abby, ed. *New to North America: Writing by U.S. Immigrants, Their Children, and Grandchildren.* Santa Cruz, CA: Burning Bush Publications, 1997.

Garcia, Pelayo. *From Amigos to Friends*. Houston: Arte Público Press, 1997.

Gernand, Renee. *The Cuban Americans*. New York: Chelsea House Publishers, 1995.

ACTIVITIES

SPEAK OUT!

Learning While You Work • Remind students about the role of lectors in the factories. What do they think about the idea of workers being read to by lectors? Discuss with them the types of workplaces where such a system might work. Then ask students to compile a list of reading material that they would like to have read to them—including a mix of fiction and nonfiction, books, and newspaper and magazine articles—and to explain their choices. Decide on an appropriate time in the classroom when a lector might be incorporated into the day, and let volunteer lectors read the material to the rest of the class as they work.

An Open Door or a Closed Door? • Pose the following discussion question to students: *Should anyone who wants to immigrate to the United States be allowed to do so?* Have them think about and refine their arguments for or against an open-door immigration policy for this country. Pair students who have differing opinions on the issue, and then let them debate the question. Set out the following rules for a good debate: take turns speaking, listen to each other without interrupting, ask questions to clarify information, and be respectful of each other's opinions. Talk about the debates. Did students' original opinions about immigration stay the same or change as a result of the discussions?

WRITE NOW!

The Poetry of Immigration • Write the following words, vertically, on the board: *America, United States, Immigration.* Charge students with the task of writing a poem based on one of these words. Ask them to think about the plays they've read, their own or others' immigration experiences, and their own feelings about living in this country. For their poems, students should begin each line with a letter in the word. The first line of a poem about America, for example, would start with a word that begins with an A; the second line would start with a word that begins with an M, and so on. Set aside time for students to share their work, and collect it in a class poetry anthology.

New Immigrants • Most of the Cubans who have come to the United States entered the country after World War II. Numbers of people originally from Central and South America, the Caribbean, and Asia—especially Vietnam, Laos, and Cambodia—have also emigrated to America during this time period. Encourage students to focus on immigrants from one particular country after World War II. After they research the political, social, and/or economic reasons that led many people from that country to leave, encourage students to write plays based on their data. You may want to let pairs or groups collaborate on plays. Let the playwrights cast and direct their plays for the class.

GETTING DOWN TO THE FACTS!

Let's Get Graphic • Assign students the task of finding statistics on the number of Cuban immigrants who have entered the United States. Tell them to locate at least six statistics from 1848 to today. Emphasize that the statistics should cover a wide range of numbers. Then have students create a bar graph or line graph to present their data. They should also create captions to describe the events in Cuba that precipitated the fluctuations in the statistics.

Leaving Cuba • Remind students that several times Castro has opened up ports such as Camarioca and Mariel to allow Cubans to leave by boat for the United States. Have students plan escape routes between a Cuban port and a Florida port. Suggest that they research factors such as climate and weather, seasons, water temperature, sea lanes, wind, and so on. Ask them to create maps featuring both Cuba and Florida to show their routes. Make sure students label cities, provinces, states, and physical features. As appropriate, their maps should contain compass roses, legends, grids, wind and ocean currents, flow lines, and vertical profiles.